You Still Don't Know My Story

Author

Shabarbara Best- Everette

Words From The Heart Publishing Company

You Still Don't Know My Story

Copyright © 2012 by Shabarbara Best- Everette

Library of Congress Cataloging-in-Publication Data

Printed in the United States of America

Words From The Heart Publishing Company books may be ordered through booksellers or by contacting:

Words From The Heart Publishing Company

www.AuthorShabarbara.com

Because of the dynamic nature of the Internet, any Web addresses or links contained in this book may have changed since publication and may no longer be valid.

Dedicated to

My Mommy,

Willie Mae Powell

Mommy,

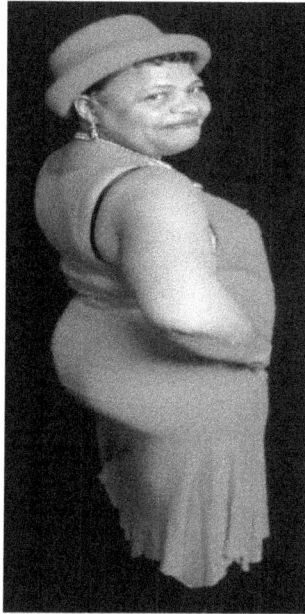

I Love You More Than You Will Ever Know!

Acknowledgements

To my **True Friends~** the ones that have stuck with me after so many years. Thank you for being my prayer warriors when I need you.

To **Bishop Johnson and the Destiny Family Christian Center~** Thank you for taking care of me and my family for the 3 years we were in El Paso, Texas.

To **Bishop Calvin Lockett and the Christ The Healer Church family~** Thank you for your many prayers when I needed it most and for being there when God performed a Miracle in my life.

To **All Of My Babies~** My Nephews, Nieces, & Goddaughter. Thanks for making me your favorite Auntie and loving me so much.

To **My God~** who has given me an Awesome gift of writing. Thank you for giving me the courage to share my story to the world. Without God I am absolutely nothing, but with Him I am more than a Conqueror!

You Still Don't Know My Story

You Still Don't Know My Story

You still don't know my story

But if I told you, it would take all day

No scratch that...even longer because I have so much to say

God has been so good to me but I've had many challenges along the way

Physically, mentally, spiritually, & emotionally but I found out that all I needed to do was obey

This lesson was a hard one to do

I'm the type of person that likes to follow my own rules

Dealing with family deaths...one by one

Dealing with my own sicknesses...the Surgeon told me I was almost gone

Constantly on edge as the next appointment approach

Feeling stress & tired and just downright broke

I'm wondering how this story will end

Because this story changes just like the wind

I don't know how my day will go from one day to the next

I try to plan my days but sometimes things come up that I don't expect

Instead of freaking out, I go with the flow

And where He leads me, that's where I will go

You still don't know my story

No matter what I've been through or what I'm going through, God will still get all of the Glory

Have You Ever?

Have you ever had a day when your mind won't rest

You're fighting within yourself

Battling your own self-made test

Going back and forth... back and forth hitting yourself in the head

When all you really want to do is just lay in the bed

Before you go to sleep, you pray that the confusion you're feeling is all a dream

But you wake up and your mind is still trap and all you want to do is blow off steam

You don't know how to release this stress without doing the wrong thing

But you're scared of the consequences that it may bring

So you suck it up as you continue to try to live right

Although it seems like it's a constant fight

Fighting against the devil and some Christians too

You really don't know whose side to be on because they both act like fools

So you choose Jesus to guide your path and to give you peace

Only He can fix what's going on with you and make your mind cease

Cease of all the evil things and focus on Him...The Heavenly Father

And He makes all those petty things disappear so it can no longer be a bother

<u>Where Do I Go From Here?</u>

Where do I go from here?

I don't know

But where you lead me

That's where I'll go

My life seems like a confusing map

But I need to find my way

I don't know what else to do

So I take it step by step every day

I'm scared to move forward so I step back

I m scared to spend money because I may lack

Surprises popping up here and there

Issues upon issues everywhere

Where do I go from here?

Can you hear me…I thought you were always near

Speak to me God tell me what to do

Oh, I forgot….. It's your timing

So I'll just wait on you

You Were Only Here For A Season

You and I were never meant to be

Not long-term just for a short while you see

You were only here for a season

No other reason than to stand as I lean

It's not what it may seem

And I'm not trying to use you or anything

But you just can't be my everything

My friend, my confidante, someone I can talk to

Vent my feelings, and then I'm through

You're like a leaf on an autumn tree

Not like the root that will stand there with me

Through thick and thin when times get tough

When the wind came, you fell because it was just too much

You were only here for a season, not a permanent stain

You would disappear as soon as it started to rain

You were only here for a season and I'm not mad nor am I sad

But I'm actually very glad

I don't have to deal with nonsense or your ever changing fad

It's time to go- kick rocks

It's time for me to get back to me and alone with my private thoughts

You Can

You can be strong

You can live long

You can dream awake

And succeed in every goal you make

You can be what God says

Follow Him and delight in His ways

You can be a soldier in the Army of the Lord

It's a war out there but there's so much to look for

You can be the conqueror you were created to be

There is no reason why you should ever accept defeat

You can fight every disease the enemy may place on you

Because by God's stripes you're healed and there's nothing the

enemy can do

You can…. You can

And with God's help you will

Just know that God is God

Let Him do His work while you stand still

I Was Chosen

I was chosen to tell you about my pain,

So you wouldn't have to go through the same

I was chosen to let you know,

The places that I've been, you don't have to go

I was chosen to be your friend

And to let you know that what you're going through is not the end

God made a way for me and He can do the same for you

Just put your trust in Him and let Him do what He's going to do

I was chosen to be a witness

He doesn't want just anything, but your very Best

Giving your best is giving your all

Make a sacrifice, don't give God something small

Delight Him by giving Him all you have

And He'll Bless you in time to come

Listen to God, Receive your calling, and He'll say, "Well Done"

He Knows

Do you know my goals, dreams, and desires?
It seemed like I was close to meeting my goal but then found out that I
was dealing with liars

Do you know the things running in my mind that won't slow down?
When you feel like cutting or beating someone to the ground

Do you know the frustration I feel when nothing goes right?
At first, I think things are going well because I can almost see the light

Do you know how it feels to see the prize but can't touch it?
Do you know how it is when you have things handed to you then taken
away immediately; no time to even enjoy it?

He knows all about my struggles, sorrow, and pain
He even knows my disappointments and my shame

He knows about every strand of hair on my head
He even knows which ones will shed

He knows what will happen before you
He has everything under control so step back because you have no clue

You don't know where to start or where to end
But when God is in the fight He will always win

I may not know but He knows
So the only thing you can do at this point is just let it go and leave it to the
Pro

A Walking Miracle

"A Walking Miracle" is what you can call me

I thought my life was over, but God had a bigger plan that even I

couldn't see

He allowed me to go through many situations and be without

Oh, what a crazy life to live

He decided to keep me safe because He had so much more to give

God allowed sickness to overtake my body, mind, and soul

Little did I know- God was still in complete control

So much has happened in my life

I wasn't supposed to be here today

But just like Job- it was only a small price I had to pay

God showed up and showed out

Healed me, changed me, and set me free

I can now say, "Devil you're defeated! I got the Victory!"

"A Walking Miracle"- Yes, that's me!

Why don't you trust God?

Remember, He's the only one who holds the Key

I Want To Be Close To You

I want to be close to you

I want to do whatever you tell me to

I want to walk in your will and in your way

I want to live right each and everyday

I want to be free of all my troubles and my pain

I don't want my living to be in vain

I want to teach and sing your Gospel all over the world

To men, women, boys, and girls

I want to be close to you

I want to feel brand new

In my spirit, my body, and my soul

I want your Holy Power to take control

Lord, I want to be close to you

I Want To Be Close To You

Please, Just Let Me Be Close To You!

I Will Miss You Daddy

I can't believe you're gone
But I'm glad you're finally home

In a place of peace
No more pain; You're now at ease

You made everyone smile even when you felt bad
You didn't want anyone pitying you or stand around you feeling sad

You never complained and you said the same thing every time
I would ask how you were... and you would always say "I'm fine"

Thank you for the time you put in on this earth
Instilling in me joy, responsibility, and self worth

Thank you for giving me Jesus and making us stay in church constantly
having to sing
Lester Best and the Bestettes traveling from place to place playing those
tambourines

Thank you for loving me unconditionally and spoiling me too
Some words you would often say...
"Shabarbara's the Baby...she can have her way"

Everyone loved those famous lemon pound cakes
You always put love in every single one you baked

Your generosity you constantly shared
You always knew how to let people know that you truly cared

You always amazed me, even after you left to be with the Lord
You were a father, a husband, a papa, and so much more

You were a man of perfection; everything had to flow
You were a friend to many and even to some you didn't really know

I couldn't have asked for a better father even if I hand- made you myself
My first love...which can never be compared to anyone else

I Will Miss You Daddy
But Now its Neicy's turn to be with you
Y'all sing in that Heavenly choir and one day I will be there too

The Joy Of The Lord

The joy of the Lord is my strength

It really doesn't matter how long the length

I could be high in the clouds or down in the dirt

He said that His joy would protect me from all harm and hurt

His joy is so special and it makes me so relaxed,

It's better than listening to the melody of a sax

The joy of the Lord is something that not everyone will understand

You have to experience it,

I know because I'm his number one fan

His joy makes me smile and laugh when problems are all around me

This same joy lets me know that I can be all that I want to be

His joy will make me strong when I am weak

His joy will put a dance in my feet

His joy will pick me up and turn me around,

It will place my feet on solid ground

The joy of the Lord is my strength,

And can be your strength, too

The decision on whether you will accept it or not is up to you

Tribute To Neicy

All of you out there doing your thing, thinking that you have time
Neicy was only 30; you need to make up in your mind

To follow Christ and live for Him
You keep talking about the future, but right now it's looking pretty dim

Neicy didn't die for her sake, but for you
She had two children to be raised; think about it, now what are you going to do?

Are you going to sit there with a blank on your face?
Wondering what to do, looking out into space?

Or are you going to run to the altar and give your life to God?
It's your decision to keep making Him take out His rod

He will continue to whip you until you answer the Call
He is God, no one like Him; He's your all and all

Don't let Neicy's death be in vain
Give your life to God and you will never be the same

Yes- I Will

Yes- I will sing your praise everywhere I go,

I will tell the world that you told me so

Yes- I will teach and preach to those who need a word

I realize that your word needs to be heard

Yes- I will dance with my partner; which is you

The devil had his turn, but I'd rather dance with someone new

Yes- I will go, like you said

I will heal the sick and raise the dead

Yes- I will do more than you have ever done

You told me that I could because I'm under the Son

Yes- I will achieve all the goals I have in my life and more

I know that I can because you have opened all the doors

Yes- I will do whatever it takes,

I know you will see me through because promises are what you will never break

<u>This Is Only A Process</u>

This is only a process that I'm going through
I can't stay there; I have too much work to do

This is only a process and it suppose to hurt
If it felt good, then I wouldn't have a reason to work

Work towards the destiny that you want me to fulfill
Work because I know it's your perfect Will

Putting things behind and forgetting my past
Stop dwelling on the things that didn't last

I have to make it through this process or it will repeat
Over and over until I pass this test not missing a single beat

God take you through a process not to hurt you but to teach you
It's up to you if you want to experience something new

You have to go through this process the right way
You can decide whether or not if this is the game you want to continue to play

This is only a process
The question is... Are you ready for God to give you the very Best?

<u>Grandma</u>

Another year has come and you've made it through a lot

Dealing with the death of your son, your friend, your confidant

Someone you could talk to every single day about any and everything

You waited every night at 10pm for the phone to ring

The last call of the day before you went to sleep

Not a long conversation but just to say goodnight... nothing too deep

Dealing with your health issues in spite of the pain

Just like your son, you never complained but always remained the same

You watch your favorite shows, do your puzzles, and your puzzle books

to pass the time

Still in good spirits when we talk while keeping him in the back of your

mine

You're a strong woman that has been through so much over the years

But "Thank God" that you're still here

Keep being the Woman of God that you are

With your Faith you will always go far

I'm honored to be your granddaughter & Malachi is happy to be your great grandson too

Keep believing and God will continue to take care of you

I Love You Grandma!

Wait On You

Dear Lord,

I am going to wait on you

I will do what you tell me to

If you tell me to wait on a special man,

I can just rely on you to hold my hand

I will wait for my calling in my life,

Although I sometimes sit around and think about how I would feel to be a wife

You know that I want a husband that's perfect in your face

I'm relying on you to choose him because I know that you have great taste

I will wait as long as it takes,

Until you tell me that special date

Different people will come, and it really doesn't matter who

I'm going to do what you tell me and...

Wait On You!

A Wake Up Call

I still can't believe that you're gone

It seems like it was the other day that I was talking to you on the phone

You were here for a season to do what you had to do

You touched lives wherever you went as you allowed God to use you

Oh what joy you brought into my life

You always knew how to make me smile

You were vivid, happy, and somewhat wild

You carried laughter with you all around

You somehow always found a way to turn frowns upside down

You were a smart and talented young man

You could play any instrument and fix anything

You were so gifted that you could even sing

You know that you were my favorite cousin

And you made it known that I was your favorite cousin too

You protected me no matter the circumstances because everyone knew what you would do

I guess this is what you call… "A Wake Up Call"

For all of us to get our house in order today

No matter your age, creed, or race

God will show Himself regardless of what you do or say

This is "A Wake Up Call" for all of those who have been taking advantage of God's unmerited favor and grace

"A Wake Up Call" for those who will never meet Him and also for those who will see Him face-to-face

Don't let another death be in vain especially those in their early years

Realize what time it is

Wake up because the coming back of God is near…in fact it's almost here

I Love You Keone!

Lamb of God

The Lamb of God- He is My King

I bow in reverence to show Him that He's worthy of the praise, the glory, the honor and everything

In spite of my sins He died on Calvary to set me free

Why you may ask? Just because He loved me

He is the Alpha and the Omega

The beginning and the end

He is so amazing but still chooses to call me His friend

And continues to bless me over and over again

There are so many words that I can say to describe Him like Healer, Provider, King of Kings, Lord of Lords, Awesome Wonder, Magnificent One, and the list will never cease

He is Omnipotent, Omnipresent, and the Prince of Peace

Thank you for being the precious Lamb of God

The Sweet Lamb of God

Thank you for being MY Lamb of God

Don't Get Too Close To Me

Don't get too close to me

I'm scared you may leave

Step away from me

I'm really hard to please

There's nothing so great about me that you should want to be attached

Be cautious because I might just attack

I don't want to be your friend

I don't want to talk to you

I want to be alone

And do what I do

If I get close you may pass away

Then I'm left broken- hearted; struggling to live day to day

I have enough friends

I don't need you

You're better off without me

And I'm better off without you too

I'm Drowning

I'm drowning
Can't seem to get to the top
I try to go up for air
Then another weight drops

Stuck in this water waves hitting me left and right
I can't seem to win it seems like a constant fight

I'm in the ocean deep
I know that I'm swimming but I can't seem to feel my feet

The sharks are out here ready to take me whole
But God you said that you're always in control

Where are you... Don't you hear me?
I'm floating farther and farther away...it's hard for me to see

Come to my rescue
Throw a buoy in
Don't let me drown in this ocean of sin

My Man Of God

You make me feel special as if I'm needed

I can tell that I'm appreciated; just by the way I'm treated

You are certainly a man of God; you show that in your walk

And you confirm this by the way you talk

Your presence among many in a crowd will still show

He's light within you is so vivid, that you can't help but to just glow

You carry yourself with distinctiveness, without the approval of anyone

You seek to please your Father

You know-God's only Son

Thank you for your prayers and all the love that you have shown so far

And when I'm down, thank you for knowing how to bring me back up to par

You are My Man of God

Made perfect, just for me

God added all of the ingredients

From the top of your head to the soles of your feet

As God was creating me, He had you in mind

He knew that you would be obedient to the Words "seek and ye shall find"

You found me just out of the blue

Although I didn't want to at first, I chose you

It was the best decision that I've ever made

My Man of God

One who loves me, but most importantly loves God and truly saved

<u>Your Love</u>

Your Love is unconditional and so true

If I didn't have your love, I wouldn't know what to do

I would be down in dumps or buried in the sand

I would desire your helping hand,

To pick me up

And take me out of the mess where I feel stuck

There are times when I take advantage of your love

I sometimes forget where my help comes from, which is from above

I always go back and ask for forgiveness

And you take me back with no bitterness

Your love is like no other love I ever imagined that I could have from anyone

And God you showed me all that Love when you gave me your only Son

Delay But Not Denied

You put it in my face and it seems real but then you take it away

You told me that I could have two babies but I don't have either one of them today

You said that you would give me double for my trouble but when will that day come?

And what I really want to know is where is it coming from?

I don't have my twins but I did get a chance to talk to my Daddy the day before he left this Earth

Although it hurts to not have my babies, knowing that my Daddy knew how much I loved him was worth more than me giving birth

I may be delayed in some things that God promised me, but I'm certainly not denied

Despite of what it may look like I am truly Blessed because I have God on my side

My Personal Thanks

I know that it's not always spoken

But I really do appreciate you

You pop up with more love and gifts

Just out of the blue

I can't "Thank You" enough for just being there

Not to be in my business, but to sincerely show that you care

You were Heaven sent and it took me until now to see

That it was none of my doing; it was God who held that key

The key to the door that is now open that had been locked for so long

To someone who wouldn't judge me, even when I do wrong

This is My Personal "Thanks" to you for being the Grandmother that Malachi can call on at anytime

Just know that you will <u>forever</u> be in our hearts and on our minds

I Love You Godmommy!

<u>Step By Step</u>

Guide me each and everyday
Direct my footsteps on my way

Take me step- by- step as I go along
Place in my heart a new song

Be there when I'm feeling low
Tell me exactly where you want me to go

Step- by- step I know that I can make it
Whatever trial I have to go through, I'm willing to take it

Step- by- step I'll make it where you are
I know that you're close by although you seem so far

Heaven is my goal and I'm willing to go all the way
But right now, I'm just asking you to guide me
Step- by- step each and everyday

<u>Mommy</u>

Mommy, there are so many things that I could say

But there aren't enough words to explain how I feel about you today

I have so many characteristics just like you

Even though I try to deny it, I do some of the same things that you do

Small beginnings is where we started and it makes me appreciate everything now

From the projects to a house- I take care of what I have because you showed me how

From food stamps to cash- but still hustling doing what I have to do to make ends meet

Making sure that my child is never without- making home cooked meals and always dressing him neat

We didn't have much

But the unconditional love you showed me was more than enough

I cherish the things and people I have because of your example

Inviting people in your home, and always giving them a sample

I cook and serve people just like you

I clean probably a little too much because that's what I saw you do

Standing by your children through the good and bad

Being available when we need you whether we're lonely, hurt, or sad

You're a great example of how a mother should be

And all I can tell you is... You mean the world to me

I Love You Mommy!

<u>Be Near</u>

Be Near me Lord

So that I may be able to know that you are there

Be Near me

So that I can see that you really care

Be Near me

So that I will know that I am good enough

To be one of the people who can feel your touch

Be Near me

So that I can smell the freshness of your soul

I know that you always have everything under control

When all the things around me are going down

I want to be able to laugh and smile instead of weep and frown

I don't want to shed another tear

I'm only asking you Lord to…

<u>Be Near</u>

You Are Always Right There

You are always right there

You've always been right there

Even when my family and so called friends were God knows where

I tried to let go and do things on my own

But you were still there even when I felt like I needed to be alone

Protecting me from the storm and the rain

Being my umbrella keeping me dry and shielding me from all the pain

There's no one greater than you

But you still take the time to be there for me

Who couldn't love a God like you?

I guess someone spiritually blind; unable to see

Keep Moving

Keep moving
Goals to reach
You can't stop now
You have to keep on moving your feet

Your mind busy
Can't even sleep
Things you should be doing
Don't be scared...take that leap

Don't be afraid to take the next step
It's not as bad as it may seem
Go ahead
Take one for the team

You will never know if you will succeed if you never try
Don't worry about your haters- they are just telling you a lie

They don't want you to accomplish what God destined for you
Stop focusing on people and do what God told you to do

Stand firm on His promises because they will forever be true
Trust and believe in God, keep moving, and He will see you through

Alpha Omega

Alpha Omega,

The beginning and the end

God will stick by you, closer than a friend

He is there when you need Him,

And even when you think you don't

He'll give you what you need,

But not always what you want

Alpha Omega,

The father of all kings

He can, without a doubt, supply you with everything

Alpha Omega,

My one, true love

He sits up high and looks down low from Heaven above

Alpha Omega,

I'm going to love Him more and more each day.

I will lean and depend on Him until I see Him face- to- face

You Are Not Alone

You are not alone in this fight

Don't worry because right now you're in the night

Day will come before you know it and new mercies you will see

Stop complaining about yesterday and use your Bible as the key

If you follow His Word, then doors will be opened for you

Believe in His Word and God will give you what is due

The more you testify, the more the devil will attack

But don't worry because God has your back

God said that the weapons will form but it won't prosper

Just do what you're supposed to do and God will conquer

You will never be alone when God is on your side

Just be who He created you to be and realize that you are the reason that He died

Struggling

I'm struggling

Struggling inside

These feelings I just can't hide

Trying to please everyone else and myself too

But it's impossible to do all the things that they expect me to do

I'm not perfect by far

So how can my life be up to par?

I need some help

I need some guidance

Who will step up with some assistance?

I can't carry this burden alone

It's just too much!

It's just wrong!

God said trouble won't last always

But I need Him today

I'm tired of struggling

It's my turn to have peace

Burdens off my shoulder with a sigh of relief

Struggling yesterday but it's all over now

Thanking God for always being there and I gratefully bow

Stop Playing

It's time to get right

Your time to leave this world could be over sooner than you think

God can take you as quickly as a blink

Stop playing around pretending to be a Christian on Sunday

And be the meanest thing that ever walked every other day

You can't live a double life and think that it's okay

You're hindering your own Blessings

You're standing in your own way

Surrender your life completely today

Don't wait until tomorrow because it may be too late

Live your life like this day is your last

Who knows?

People are leaving this world so very fast

A Good Wife

I'm here again and I'm not sure why

But I do know that I can't just sit around and constantly cry

I've tried to be a good wife and do what I'm supposed to do

But no matter what I choose, I can't seem to please you

I know I'm not who you used to have and that should be great in your eyes

But it looks like I was blind because I didn't see your disguise

You masqueraded yourself as the perfect man

So I thought things would go according to my plan

I'm not sure if it's the devil attacking or if God is putting us through a test

But I know that I told you that I was only looking for the very best

You lied to me when you pretended to change

You knew I would stay and my plans to leave would be rearranged

My life has been crazy and you knew this in advance

But yet you take me through hell again- my life in a circle of a dance

You claim you love me but you must not really know what true love is

It's not a game played between two little kids

So you better grow up and do what you're supposed to do as a man of God before it's too late

Don't wait until I'm gone to realize your mistakes

If you keep taking me for granted and taking advantage of me

Then wife #2 will be gone, along with everyone else that you pushed away or just decided to leave

I Never Would Have Made It

I never would have made it if it wasn't for your grace
There's nothing like your love or your warm embrace

Your grace is more than I could have ever asked for
And your mercy just keep opening up doors

You are such an understanding patient God
There are several times I thought you would bring out your rod

But you never gave up on me no matter how many times I messed up
You saw pass my disguise and knew that I wasn't tough

I messed up on purpose at times and you still took me in your arms
You continued to protect me from all hurt and harm

You held me until I could get my mind back together again
You reminded me that you are still my closest friend

You put me back on track every time I fell
You reminded me that no matter what it looks like… All Is Well!

I Didn't Ask For This

I didn't ask for this… one may say

I was hoping that my life would go a totally different way

I didn't ask to be poor, rejected, or abused

I didn't ask to be molested or used

I didn't ask to come to this world to be treated like dirt

I may not be perfect but I now know what I'm worth

I didn't ask to be taken for granted by family or so called friends

I could tell you all the things that have happened to me but I'm not sure where I should begin

I didn't ask to be a single parent and do everything on my own

I had to choose to get rid of him or do everything alone

I didn't ask for a lot of things but it happened for a reason

There's a time for everything good and bad but I have to wait for my season

It won't be bad always just wait to see where you are being lead

Keep holding on because there are better days ahead

Why Do I Keep Trying

Why do I keep on trying?

It's not working no matter what I say

I feel like I'm stuck in a rut every single day

I wake up, pray, and start my daily tasks

I pray because God said all I had to do was ask

So I ask for guidance and patience to say the least

But somehow things get turned upside down so by the end of the day I'm asking God for peace

Peace in my home, my mind, and my body too

Peace for my family and friends that somehow we can come together and stick like glue

Why do I keep on trying to be the person that I feel will make God proud

I keep trying because I'm scared to be alone; I need God to stick around

I keep trying because Heaven is my goal and I can't stay in this place

I keep trying because one day I will see God face to face

Unforgiveness

Unforgiveness is something that plagued me on a regular basis and it was hard to release

I know that I'm not Christ but God commanded us to forgive so that we could have peace

People hating me for no reason at all; those that I knew well

If you left it up to them a lie is what they would tell

Trying to cover up the real reason that they despised me

Little petty things, nick picky, just because I'm not who they wanted me to be

I choose not to kiss up to anyone no matter who they are

You can love me or hate me; I'm blunt from the very start

I don't have time to please you, everyone else, and myself too

That's just too much work

I won't have the chance to be Super Mom, Loving Wife, Author, and all the other things that I like to do

Forgive me if I don't focus on you everyday

But I just have to do things my way

I can't continue to harbor unforgiveness because of the way you have treated me

I'm letting go, forgiving you for your faults against me, and being totally free

All I can do is pray for you and your state of mind

And I will continue to be myself...sincere and kind

Lead Me

Lead me Guide me along the way

Lord if you lead me I will not stray

That's a song that I used to hear during devotional service but I didn't understand it until now

I need you and only you because I want you to show me how

How to live the Godly life that I read about

The Godly life that makes people want to shout

The Godly life that I know I should live

Being there for others is nice and it's great that I love to give

But the reality is this... only giving won't hold your spot the Heavenly line

You have to give your heart to God; it goes beyond you being kind

People will take advantage of your tender heart

They will use you up until you have no more

But God gives us wisdom and discernment so that you will know how to soar

I'm Tired

I'm tired and frustrated beyond measure

I can't seem to have a single day of pleasure

There's always something going on in my life

I feel like I constantly have to fight

I'm tired of fussing, being pissed off, and just angry

God step in and Save Me!

Give me that peace that I've been praying for

Please God I need you to open a window or crack the door

Let me hear your voice; soothe me with your power

Please give me a break even if it's only for one hour

Please come to my rescue because I'm tired

I'm so hot- I feel like I'm on fire

I feel like I will explode at any time

If someone else say anything to me, I will SNAP at a drop of a dime

Lord please give me peace

I need your peace

I need this anger to cease

Take Your Hands Off My Child

You thought you could take my child and use him for your glory

But Satan you won't win this battle

Maybe you forgot about my story

Did you forget the many deaths in my family?

Did you forget the Cancer you plagued on me?

God delivered me from the stress, pain, and misery

He said by His stripes I am healed so you will never be the death of me

God will decide when it's my time to leave this earth

So devil take your hands off my child

Yes- I also know what he's worth

When God decided to give me Malachi, He told me that he was my gift

And I had to teach him the difference between Blessings and this world's filth

Devil you thought that if you used the closest person in my life to stress me that you won

That was so far from the truth because this fight has just begun

Now you have a war on your hands because God made promises to me about this child and He can't lie

So step back devil, take your hands off, turn yourself around, and say goodbye

My Scars

My Scars do define who I am and what I've been through

You're looking at me now but you have no clue

No clue about the surgeries, recovery, or pain in the past

My Scars remind me that it may hurt for a minute but it won't last

My Scars show you ugly marks but it has made me a more beautiful person inside and out

My Scars tell you what I'm really all about

My physical scars show my cuts and bruises of the journey of my life

It shows that I may have been hit but I won the fight

My Scars says if I can go through this, then I can go through that

Even though they may not be easy to look at

But it's who I was and it's who I am now

God always brought me through somehow

My Scars have transformed me into something better than I knew that I could be

A more humble person, reliable person, and someone who is now free

My Scars have made me want to be better, talk better, act better, and make better choices

It has made me realize that I shouldn't dwell on petty things but I should use my voice

Use my voice to share with others the importance of their life

That they need to take care of themselves and stop all the strife

My Scars are there to remind me that by His stripes I am healed

And no matter how many scars I get, God's Glory will Always be revealed

Praise Without A Voice

Devil you tried to mess with me

You tried to take my voice away so I couldn't praise God

You thought that I would silently sit back and just nod

You didn't want me to share my testimony with the world to show how good God has been to me

You thought you would win this battle and I would just let things be

I may be silent now but this will just give me more desire to speak

Look at me...I still have the Victory; I'm not weak

God told me to lean not to my own understanding and acknowledge Him in all His ways

And that's what I live by from day to day

I can praise God without a voice

He gave me limbs so I can wave my hands

I can smile; I can do my dance

I am more than a Conqueror and in Him I trust

Nothing you can do devil will ever be enough

I stand firm in my belief; God is my King

And no matter what I go through

I still owe Him my everything

This is only a process; temporary so I'm taking it step by step

Voice or no voice... And I am confident in knowing that God will be my help

Voice or no voice...I will forever praise your name

And I will forever encourage everyone in my path to do the same

Fake People

I need consistency in my life

I'm tired of fake people stabbing me in the back with a knife

Smiling in my face now

Then talking about me like I'm a fat cow

Not knowing what to expect

Not knowing what to do next

You sit back as if everything is okay

Then as soon as I turn around you have something to say

It's ridiculous how people act at times

But it is what it is so I'll be just fine

Looking for people to do what's right is a joke

It will never happen…maybe when they're asleep because it won't happen if they're woke

Life is full of many ups and downs

Life is full of many characters and clowns

People that will be there until the end

People to step in and be your closest friend

Then there are people who just hate you just because you're you

And there's nothing that you can do

You Can't Shake Me

You can't shake my faith

I'm a believer

There's too much at stake

You're nothing but a deceiver

God has me in His hands

So stop pushing me

Don't bump me

Take your filthy hands off of me

You can't shake me devil

You can do this, that, or whatever

God will always be in control of every situation

You can't wait for Him to go on a vacation

It won't happen, He's always at work

So you might as well stop being a jerk

Move on with your life because my life is in God's hands

You can try to shake me but I will continue to stand

You won't win

You can't win

The battle is already won

You have to remember that I'm a child of the Holy One

It Will Get Better

It will get better

Don't worry about what it looks like right now

God has everything under control

Take your hands off and bow

Bow down to God and let Him do His work

The more you do the more you will get hurt

I'm so glad that morning has to come and it won't stay dark

God is gracious and He has my heart

He knows what I want and what I need

He always has me in mind so I have to succeed

He told me to speak those things as if it was so

And I take Him at His Word and I have to let you know

God is Awesome!

He's My Healer, My Protector, and My Guide

I'm never alone

He's always by my side

It will get better no matter what it is

Stand on God's word and believe everything He promised because you are His

The Facts

I'm a living witness that God still performs Miracles because He did it for me

Some Doctors don't know it, but Faith is not something that you can see

My Faith said that I was healed and God showed me just that

Doctors have science but God removed all of the facts

The Facts were...the Cancer was back and I couldn't believe it

The facts were... it was bigger and surgery was needed

The facts were... that I would continue to have pain

The facts were... that I needed to remove my breasts but I would never feel the same

The facts were... that Chemotherapy was in my future plans

But the fact is...God has All Power in His hands

The doctors could see what was going on inside

But what they didn't know was God's Word had to abide

Although the Cancer showed on the Mammograms and Ultrasounds

When the Surgeon went to look for it, it was nowhere to be found

God promised that He wouldn't put more on me than I could bear

So when I needed Him, He was right there

That fact is God's Grace and Mercy is more than what I deserve

I am so Grateful that I have a God that will forever keep His Word

You Can't Break My Spirit

I've been through too much

And done too many things for me to just give up

I have to trust God's word no matter how hard the test

I have to keep reminding myself that this is only a process

The devil is trying to keep me down and break my spirit

The devil doesn't know that I will not budge; not one bit

I've seen God do some magnificent things over the years

I can't stop trusting Him now, time is drawing near

This is a journey that I have to take

No matter how hard it gets, I have to do this for my sake

He's still my all and all

Although I sometimes break down and fall

God picks me up, brushes me off, and tells me to ascend

And He reminds me that this is not the end

God has me in the palms of his hands

You may break my spirit at the moment but I will get up again and again and again

Cancer Free

The Doctor standing in unbelief

Where could this thing be?

For some reason I can't see

The mass that was so big have somehow disappeared

Even the small masses are no longer here

What is going on? I don't understand

What you don't understand Doctor is that it's in God's hands

He took that Cancer away

No surgery for me today

He already removed ever bad cell within

He cares for me

He's my best friend

Cancer you are nothing compared to Jesus Christ

He said by His stripes I'm healed because He already paid the Price

Devil, that thing you plagued on me

God took it away and now I'm Cancer Free

My Secret

You're not suppose to touch me there

Your hand shouldn't even be close to my underwear

You're suppose to protect me but instead you take advantage of me 3 different times while I'm sleep

I know that I should have told someone but this was a secret that I had to keep

Not for my safety but for yours

If I would have told my Daddy, then your life would have been over before you could promise not to do it anymore

I never understood why you brought so many little girls to your house to treat them like your little toys

For some reason, I can't remember you ever picking up any boys

Maybe I should have said something

Maybe I could have saved someone else

But at that time I had to think about myself

I had to choose between telling someone and saving my father from committing a crime

There was no way I could have allowed him to kill you and then have to do time

I've kept this secret for far too long- every since my childhood

Years had passed and it still affected me in my adulthood

So I had to realize that it was time to move on and forgive you for the things you did to me

I didn't do it for you, but because I needed to be free

My Secret was hidden from everyone but now it's in the opening

Maybe someone else will be brave enough to share their secret; at least that's what I'm hoping

www.ingramcontent.com/pod-product-compliance
Lightning Source LLC
Chambersburg PA
CBHW081638040426
42449CB00014B/3364